Canticles of Light

for upper-voice choir, SATB choir, and orchestra

Vocal score

MUSIC DEPARTMENT

OXFORD
UNIVERSITY PRESS

OXFORD
UNIVERSITY PRESS

Great Clarendon Street, Oxford OX2 6DP, England
198 Madison Avenue, New York, NY10016, USA

Oxford University Press is a department of the University of Oxford.
It furthers the University's aim of excellence in research, scholarship,
and education by publishing worldwide

ISBN 978-0-19-343288-8

Music and text origination by
Barnes Music Engraving Ltd., East Sussex
Printed in Great Britain on acid-free paper by
Halstan & Co. Ltd., Amersham, Bucks.

English translations by George Chukinas © Oxford University Press 2000
Cover design by Philip Atkins

Canticles of Light is scored for upper-voice choir, SATB choir, 2 flutes, oboe, 2 clarinets in B flat, bassoon, 2 horns in F, tubular bells, timpani, and strings. If the requisite forces are not available, the wind and brass parts may be substituted with a reduction for organ, arranged by Antony Baldwin. All orchestral material, including the organ reduction, is available to hire from the publisher.

In addition, the accompaniment exists in a version for organ and tubular bells alone, prepared with the help of Sarah Baldock. This is available to purchase from the publisher, ISBN 0-19-335538-8.

Contents

Composer's note

Canticles of Light is a setting of three Latin Hymns from the *Liturgia Horarum*. The first two, which are dark in character, are evening hymns that entreat God for protection and comfort through the night. The music lightens for the final hymn, a song for the morning, which expresses the belief that, with God's help, the light of day will encourage new strength and hope.

Bob Chilcott

In performance, the upper-voice choir can be situated away from the mixed choir and orchestra, to give distance to the quasi-plainsong melodies that they sing.

Commissioned in the year 2000 by Winchester Music Club in celebration
of the 75th Anniversary of its founding by Sir George Dyson

Canticles of Light

1. *Te lucis ante terminum*

BOB CHILCOTT

Hymn at Compline
from *Liturgia Horarum*

* *Before the end of day,*

* Translation by George Chukinas © Oxford University Press 2000.

creator of all things, we ask you . . .

te per_ so-por- em sen - ti -ant,_ tu-am-que sem - per glo-ri-am

S.
A.

-ent, te per so-por-em sen - ti - ant, tu-am-que sem-per glo - ri -

T.
B.

let us feel you near while sleeping, *and let us celebrate always your eternal glory in the light of the new dawn.*

vi-ci - na lu - ce con - ci -nant._

- am vi-ci - na lu - ce con - ci - nant.

mp dolce

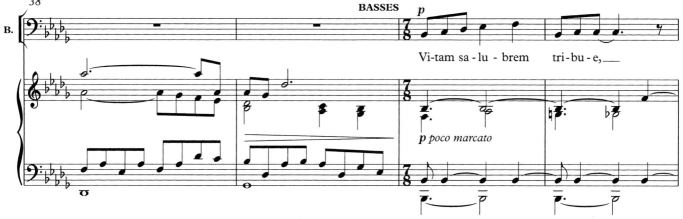

B.

BASSES *p*

Vi-tam sa - lu - brem tri-bu - e,_

p poco marcato

Grant our bodies health,

restore our strength,

...be illuminated by your brightness.

Do all this, omnipotent Father,

through Jesus Christ the Lord ...

6

...who reigns with you and the Holy Ghost forever.

2. *Christe, qui, splendor et dies*

Hymn at Compline
from *Liturgia Horarum*

you who roll away the shadows of the night,

who bestowed the light of light, *telling of the light to come for the blessed.*

101

105

S. Pre - ca - mur, sanc - te Do - mi - ne, hac noc - te__ nos cus -

A. Pre - ca - mur, sanc - te Do - mi - ne, hac noc - te__ nos cus -

T. Pre - ca - mur, sanc - te Do - mi - ne, hac noc - te__ nos cus -

B. Pre - ca - mur, sanc - te Do - mi - ne, hac noc - te__ nos cus -

We pray, Holy Lord,   *that you watch over us this night;*

109

- to - di - as; sit no - bis in te re - qui - es,_____ qui -

- to - di - as; sit no - bis in te re - qui - es,_____ qui -

- to - di - as; sit no - bis,_____ no - bis in te re - qui - es, qui -

- to - di - as; sit no - bis,_____ no - bis in te re - qui - es, qui -

let us find rest in you,   *and grant*

113

dim. *p*

-e - tas ho - ras tri - bu - e.

dim. *p*

-e - tas ho - ras tri - bu - e.

dim. *p*

-e - tas ho - ras tri - bu - e.

dim. *p*

-e - tas ho - ras tri - bu - e.

p espress.

us peaceful hours.

117

pp cresc.

Som - no si

pp cresc.

Som - no si dan - tur

pp cresc.

Som-no si dan - tur o-cu-li,

pp cresc.

Som - no_____ si dan - tur o-cu-

Though our eyes be given over to sleep,

Let our hearts be filled with you through the night;

and with

your right hand protect the faithful who cherish you.

129

_in - si - di - an - tes re - pri - me,___ gu-ber - na_

_in - si - di - an - tes re - pri - me,___ gu-ber - na_

_De-fen - sor nos - ter,   as - pi - ce,___   gu-ber - na tu - os_

_De-fen - sor nos - ter,   as - pi - ce,___   gu-ber - na tu - os_

Look upon us, our protector,   check those who beset us,   and guide your servants . . .

133

_tu - os fa-mu-los,   quos san - gui-ne___ mer - ca - tus es.   Sit, Chris - te,_

tu - os fa-mu-los,   quos san-gui-ne   mer - ca - tus es.   Sit, Chris - te,

_fa-mu-los,   quos san-gui-ne___ mer - ca - tus es.   Sit, Chris - te,_

fa-mu-los,   quos san-gui-ne   mer - ca - tus es.   Sit, Chris - te,

. . . whom you have redeemed with your blood.   _Glory be to you Christ,_

14

3. *O nata lux de lumine*

Hymn at Laudes

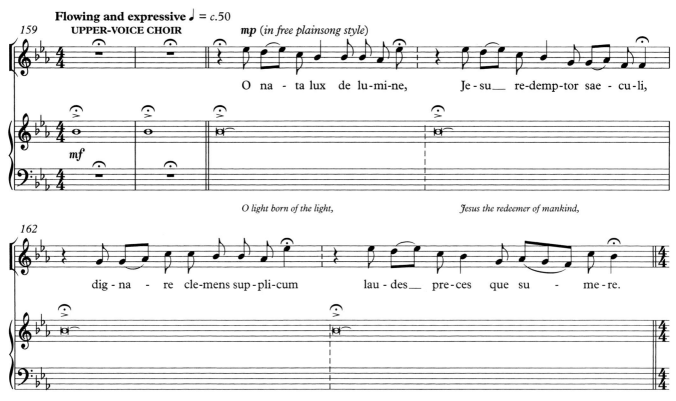

. . . the praises and prayers of your suppliants.

You who once stooped

to take on human form . . .   . . . on behalf of those who were lost,

grant that our weary limbs . . .   . . . find a resting place in you.

cor - por - is.

cor - por - is.

cor - por - is.

cor - por - is.

mf espress.

UPPER-VOICE CHOIR

mp (in free plainsong style)

O na - ta lux de lu-mi-ne,   Je-su__ re-demp-tor sae - cu-li,

dim.   *p* > *mf*

O light born of the light,   Jesus redeemer of mankind,

rit. e dim. al fine

dig-na - re cle-mens sup-pli-cum,   lau-des__ pre-ces que su - me-re.

mp   *p*

kindly deign to accept . . .   . . . the praises and prayers of your suppliants.